The Change Within Me

TyJuan Davis

<u>DEDICATION</u>

This book is dedicated to the haters who
encourage me to do what I'm doing faster.
The critics who motivate me
to do what I'm doing better.
My supporters who help me remain
focused on fulfilling my purpose.
And CHRIST who strengthen me
to do all things

Contents

<u>ACKNOWLEDGMENTS</u>

Giving honor to the Holy Trinity;

God The Father, Jesus The Son and the Holy Spirit

which are responsible for the change within me.

Special acknowledgements going out

to my Cloud of Witnesses in heaven;

Supt. Roy "Paw Paw" Davis Sr., Thelma "Mema" Davis,

& Joshua and Vernell Stidham...

My grandparents **Joe and Katherine Mason**

both living in their golden years of life...

Special thanks to my parents

Lisa and Ron Stidham & Apostle Bill & VaLisa Davis.

While I'm at it, one of the people responsible for helping me

while The Change Within Me occurred, my pastor and friend

Don Crowley and his wife **Sherry Crowley.**

My publisher **Jerica Wortham.**

THE CHANGE WITHIN ME

God I give you the credit for

THE CHANGE WITHIN ME,

Which allows me to even love my enemies.

I put away childish things now that I'm grown.

I'm even able to humble myself and admit when I'm wrong.

My mind is being renewed which creates more self-control.

My flesh is being purged which is making me whole.

THE CHANGE WITHIN ME is bringing unity,

So that I can now promote peace in the community.

It allows me to inspire others to follow your lead.

It grants me faith in my time of need.

Jesus you gave your life on Calvary,

And then you rose from the dead and set the captive free.

Having the Holy Spirit gives me power over evil and death.

So I acknowledge the Holy Trinity in all my ways,

As God transforms me and order my steps.

GIVE YOU THE WORLD

I'm not the best with words,

But mama if I could, I'd GIVE YOU THE WORLD.

I appreciate the love you've given throughout the years,

You've loved me unconditionally throughout the tears.

There were times I was full of despair,

But you gave me strength by letting me know you care.

You are my world, without you I wouldn't have made it,

So I want to let you know you're appreciated.

I'm a firm believer of giving credit where credit is due,

So I had to start this book by saying thank you.

If this book is a success and makes me rich,

You'll be the first one I'll pamper with gifts.

You've instilled in me morals and values when I was a kid,

That will remain in my heart as long as I live.

So if somehow you don't get to see me become a success,

I will still remain blessed.

Mama since I've became a man I understand the sacrifice,

You made to provide me with the best of life.

So in return I'm going to GIVE YOU THE WORLD,

Mama you are worth more than diamonds and pearls.

YOU'RE THE MAN

Though We Haven't Always Seen Eye To Eye With Each Other,

I Still Want To Appreciate You Like I Appreciate My Mother.

For You Were The Firm Hand Who Didn't Spare The Rod,

Who Made Us Go To Church And Take Time Out For God.

You Were The Bread Winner Who Kept The Lights On,

I Don't' Know How You Did It, But You Stayed Strong.

You Taught Me How To Live Life With No Regrets,

Therefore Pops You Will Always Have My Respect.

At Times I Didn't Realize How Lucky I Was

That You Cared To Discipline Me With Your Tough Love.

You Taught Me How To Respect All The Grown Folks,

You Made Sure When It Was Cold That I Had A Warm Coat.

You Kept Me In Check And For That I'm Glad,

If It Wasn't For You I Would've Ended Up In A Body Bag.

I Know You've Never Been Too Sentimental,

So I'm Going To Go Ahead And Keep It Simple.

Thank You For Bringing Me Into This World,

And Not Killing Me When I Got On Your Nerves.

So I Want To Take The Time To Say I Understand,

And Dad You're The Man.

KATHERINE MASON

K- is for the Knowledge you share that remains true

A- is for the Anointing that God has placed on you

T -is for the Tenderness that you show to your kids

H-is for the Holiness in the way you live

E -is for the Experience you gain through 75 years on earth

R- is the Respect you deserve for putting God first

I -is for the Intelligence that you share with those who listen

N- is for the News of Hope you give to those in prison

E -is for the Example you set as a mother, daughter & wife

M- is for the Missionary you are for Jesus Christ.

A- is for All the secrets people have told you to keep.

S- is for the Strength you display when feeling weak.

O- is for you Overcoming the trbulations you have faced.

N- is for New life you will receive when you finish the race.

MY MEMA

MY MEMA cooked Sunday dinner and welcomed everyone,
For if you went to church you were able to come.
Some people at church sat in the front, others in the back,
But MY MEMA would be on the second pew with a fancy hat.
MY MEMA was a sharp dresser, she had the finest clothes,
She had the personality to draw everyone close.
You would notice MY MEMA playing the tambourine,
Two-stepping to the song she chooses to sing.
MY MEMA was a very good grandmother, mother, and wife,
she was married to my grandpa 55 years of their life.
My dad's mom's biggest joy came from serving the Lord,
So she was a sweet lady with a voice sure to be heard.
MY MEMA bought me my first pair of Nikes when I was eleven, and when
I was 26 MY MEMA was called to heaven.
When I was 22 I ended up going to prison,
And I never saw my MEMA again while she was living.
To this day I still deal with remorse and regret,
Because I wanted to tell her "THANK YOU" before her death.
However, I know she's in heaven having happy days,
So she no longer suffers instead she's giving God praise.
I've learned a valuable lesson,
Our love ones that are alive are truly blessings.
One day either you or them will be gone,
But through their families a legacy will go on.
So through this book MY MEMA will live,
And I will pass on the love she gave me to my kids

THANK YOU "PAWPAW"
Superintendent
ROY DAVIS SR.

Grandpa I want to thank you for being the man you were and possessing, the good qualities that made you such a blessing. A lot of people had the privilege of being directed in your path, enlightened by your words of wisdom and your hearty laugh. Thank you "PawPaw" for the dedication you possessed which kept you from ceasing to pray. I seriously believe this is the reason you live a long quality life of 91 years. I take time to admire you for the courage, discipline, strength and devotion to Christ, it took to have to face the challenge. We saw you conquer every challenge and defeat every devil you go against. So we Thank God for you. Also Thank You ROY DAVIS for your diligence to study the word and show yourself approved. This allowed Jesus to build their faith. This caused numerous mountains to be moved. It's an honor to call you my grandfather for many reasons I can't name them all. I want to keep your name living forever and many other people day. When I think of black history month you're my hero. When I came in this world you were the same man I knew until God called you home February 24th 2018 been by my side to catch me if I were to fall. Another reason is the for the war you have endured, but throughout the battle the love of God has kept your heart pure. You have withstood situations that would've made most people crumble. Through it all have kept your eyes on God and remained humble. All good things are sent down from above. So this is my dedication to say" Thank you PAWPAW."

PASTOR CROWLEY

P- is for the Practical way you Preach without holding back.

A-is for the Awareness God gives you to see the devil's Attacks.

S -is for the Service you provide to the Saints

T -is for the Tambourine you use to give God Thanks.

O -is for the Obedient way in which you Observe God's Word

R -is for the Reverence you have in Regards to Jesus our Lord.

C -is the Character you are and Courage that keeps you alive.

R -is for your Respect for holiness and Righteousness you don't hide.

O -is for your Openness as you Offer what God gives you.

W -is for the Wonderful and amazing Works God is going to do.

L -is for the Listener you are as you shepherd and Lead this flock.

E -is for the Energy you have that seems to never stop, or end.

Y -is You are my pastor, and You are my friend.

NOW OR NEVER

At this point in my life it's either
NOW OR NEVER.
I'm physically fit as well as mentally sharp and clever.
I can't undo the mistakes of the past,
But I'd be a fool to let life slip from my grasp.
So from now on I got to make every minute count,
As well as calculate every dollar into a larger amount.
I have had a taste of living it up lavish.
I'm 32 now and I should've been established.
Growing up I unfortunately made a lot of bad decisions,
I know I wouldn't still be living if I didn't have a mission.
All the things I've been through just made me stronger.
It's NOW OR NEVER,
And I can't wait any longer.
Nobody knows when God's going to open the gate.
So my head is up and my feet pointed straight.
Dissect my lineage and realize my pedigree.
I'm Popeye full of spinach and Bruno can't stop me.
So it's NOW OR NEVER!
The clock is ticking.
I'm looking for the best shot against the opposition.
Maybe I'll drive in the paint and hit them with a hook.
That will occur when you see who wrote this year's hottest book.
Then a few months later watch me get a deal.
I'm not arrogant but I know I got skills.
I have dreams of owning my own clothing line.
Since God is for me and it's
NOW OR NEVER,
Can't nobody stop my shine.

1 NIGHT

1 NIGHT I stayed up thinking about my life,
Thinking about the things I've done and what I haven't done right.
As I thought I began to feel empty and knew exactly why,
Because as I sat in my cell I realized life was passing me by.
Everybody wants to be cool and have riches and gold,
But me I've been in and out of prison since I was 16 years old.
I remember going to school making good grades,
Having visions of being successful and getting paid.
Then I started making choices that wouldn't help me succeed,
Like selling this boy pepper and telling him its weed.
Next thing I knew I was looking at girls with a different look,
Then I began spending more time with friends then in my books.
Soon I was getting high and feeling up girls' skirts,
Instead of concentrating on school assignments and homework.
So I went from getting all A's and passing,
To being the class clown who had everybody laughing.
The teachers didn't like this,

Especially when they were trying to speak.
So I started getting suspended every other week.
In 10th grade I got snitched on for bringing a knife to school,
Probably a good thing because I planned to cut that fool.
Two months later I went to jail for something my cousin and I did.
In 1998 went to the boy's ranch with the other bad kids.
I got out after 6 months and still didn't know how to act,
Because that next year I ended up going to max.
The judge didn't adjudicate me so I can say I was blessed,
But the outcome still made my mom cry and stress.
I still graduated high school but instead of walking across the stage,
I took my picture from right outside a cage.
When I got out at the end of 2000 I moved to a different state,

In hopes that I could turn my life around and learn from my mistakes.
So I started working and saving money to get on my feet.
I got an apartment and a car but neither one was cheap.
Seemed like no matter how hard I worked I still struggled.
So 1 NIGHT I decided I was going to hustle.
I began selling crack and weed to get extra money.
Next thing I was balling and getting love from all the honeys.
The extra attention and the lifestyle made me feel like a star,
Until 1 NIGHT I was set up at a local bar.
Due to some white snitch and some weed,
Everything was taken from me.
From that point I was the black sheep of the family.
Grandma was cool but now I am grown,
And as they say God bless the child with his own.
I needed money so I went back on the block,
And once again I had a pocket full of crack rocks,
Because weed was too bulky and the smell was too loud.
I learned my lesson when I got stuck in the crowd.
I was getting money and things were going smooth,
Until 1NIGHT I was out to late making moves.
The police scooped up on me and I gave them a fake name.
They didn't buy it and I got caught up in the game.
The story goes on but I've told you enough for 1 NIGHT.
So if you want to hear the rest you got to sit tight.

I'M A MAN NOW

I'M A MAN NOW and realize a woman's heart is not a toy.

I realize the difference between a man and a boy.

A man is willing to work to put a smile on his woman's face,

Because he knows how much she's worth and that nobody can take her place.

You're the type of woman that makes me a better man.

That's why we walk side by side holding hands.

At this brief moment we may be miles apart.

However, were still bonded together because you're in my heart.

It was a smart decision when we met to take things slow.

Otherwise I may never have learned what I needed to know.

Things such as what to do when you're mad at the world.

Or the secret fears you had when you were just a girl.

I admit when I was young I was a mischievous little boy,

but I'M A MAN NOW and my heart is full of joy.

ATTRACTION

The ATTRACTION I feel draws me deeper with each step I take,

Assuring me this is destiny and we are soulmates.

A woman like you is priceless because all the love you give.

So I want you to be my wife and the mother of my kid's.

I know it's not often when I take the time to express the way I feel,

But never doubt that I love you and that my love for you is real.

A strong woman goes beyond the barrier of a man's incarceration.

We know love never fails and conquers all situations.

Your name is embedded in my heart with bold letters.

So I'll give you my last name in hopes that we'll always be together.

WHEN I SEE YOU AGAIN

I've never proclaimed to be too macho or hard.

However, as a real man it's up to me to step up and take charge.

When someone gets hurt it's easy for them to pass the blame.

However, without accepting responsibility nothing will ever change.

So I'm going to swallow my pride and admit I was wrong.

I'm letting go of all the resentment so we can move on.

Rather we move forward together or separate forever.

At least after getting things off my chest I will feel better.

What is done is done so there's no need to relive the pain,

However, there would never be a rainbow if it didn't rain.

For quite a while I've sat in silence and have waited,

Trying to decipher feelings which are so complicated.

I ask myself can we at least be friends?

I'm unsure of how I'll respond WHEN I SEE YOU AGAIN.

A couple of things could happen when I look in your eyes.

Either physical stimulation could occur, my nature may rise.

All the feelings that I've accepted could rush to the surface.

I could get butterflies in my stomach and begin to feel nervous.

I may realize what we once shared has come to an end,

So I wait to the day WHEN I SEE YOU AGAIN.

FIGHT TO THE END

I will not fold, break, nor bend,

Because I'm determined to FIGHT TO THE END.

I will not hold anything back. I will use all my strength,

So truly it doesn't matter what or who I go against.

I've been an underdog since I came out my mama's womb.

So I will fight till the day I get put in the tomb.

I will fight for freedom of my ideas to be expressed in new ways.

Unfazed by others opinions or what they may say.

I will fight to be looked at as more than a just a statistic,

But instead as a brother who is strong, intelligent and gifted.

I will FIGHT TO THE END for those who feel rejected.

I'll let them know only as individuals, we should be accepted.

If we are not accepted for who we are why be accepted at all?

If we don't stand for something we will always fall.

I'm going to fight for the women who gave us all birth,

As well as the next generation who inherits the Earth.

I will fight for a better future then what my past has been,

But most importantly I'm going to

!!! FIGHT TO THE END !!!

MY OASIS

I was all alone treading thru valleys & mountains,

I saw so many vultures I stopped counting.

I was on the verge of dying from thirst,

Or the heat of the sun, whichever came first.

So I was walking with extreme caution,

My body was threatening to shut down due to exhaustion.

I was delirious and beginning to get weak,

My body was going numb; I couldn't feel my feet.

I couldn't walk one more step, I'd lost my drive,

I was about to give up and close my eyes.

Just then to my surprise I heard a soft voice say,

"Keep going and everything will be ok."

Then I felt some cold water go down my throat,

At that moment miraculously I regained hope.

That's when you rejuvenated me from inside out.

It was as though you resuscitated my body like mouth to mouth.

It was then I realized your love was contagious,

Cause you quenched my thirst and became

!!! MY OASIS !!!

NO REVOCATION OF MY PROBATION

I came to Oklahoma on vacation,
Now I'm facing revocation of my probation.
I did literally 4 ½ years on an 8year sentence.
Dec. 31st 2013 was the day my stint in prison was finished.
Now once again I'm in county oranges with 7 yrs. over my head.
Last month I was with my girl in our queen size bed.
The DA feels like my probation should be revoked.
Since I didn't catch a felony charge I feel like it's joke.
I feel like this is the definition of double jeopardy.
So I'm on my knees asking the Good Lord to help me.
They say come on vacation leave on probation and that's no lie.
With all these petty laws I see why.
So I'm leaving Oklahoma and I'm not coming back.
I'm moving to a different location on the map.
I was only out 10 months I couldn't even make it 12.
Now I'm facing a probation violation while I sit in a jail cell.
I got charged with a misdemeanor and failed my UA,
& I got 2 months behind on the court fines I had to pay.
None of this is really enough to send me back to prison,
But if I do go back I'm not even tripping,
At least I'll be able to cross state lines and take a vacation.
I do know one thing, next time there will be
!! NO REVOCATION OF MY PROBATION !!

THE 1ST FEW MONTHS

THE 1ST FEW MONTHS are hard when you get out of prison,
Because you want to catch up on the things you've been missing.
The first few days you're going to want to chill,
Be around family and eat a home cooked meal.
So either you'll stick with the lady that's been riding with you,
Or you get dressed up and go find someone new.
Seeing your family will definitely make you smile,
And of course you'll go see the homies you haven't seen in a while.
They'll probably ask you what all you need.
Then take you out to drink and smoke some weed.
You'll come home to baby buzzed up with your head spinning,
She'll be so happy you're out of prison, she'll still be grinning.
The next week you'll begin to notice your pockets are light,
And you can't just go out and buy the things you would like.
So you'll begin to put in applications one after the next.
After a while you may get frustrated & begin to stress.
THE 1ST FEW MONTHS you're dedicated to finding a job.
Then you begin thinking of someone you can rob.
Your kids are hungry and you need some bucks.
You're walking while your homies have new cars and trucks.
Your patience is wearing thin and the blocks calling your name.
You now got a job but you rather be selling cocaine,
Lbs. of weed or even maybe ice.
You used to get paid everyday now in a month just twice.
Sadly, your check from your job barely pays your bills.
The struggle of THE 1ST FEW MONTHS is real.
Seems like no matter what you do you can't win,
Because you want money but you don't want to go back to the pen.
Your family notices your struggles and missed you so,
They give you some money and advise you to spend it slow.
You did your time like a soldier behind the fence,
But these 1ST FEW MONTHS seems to be taking all your strength.

IM JUST A VESSEL

I realize I'M JUST A VESSEL in need of being molded.

So Lord cleanse me thoroughly so I will be devoted,

To your will, understanding, knowledge and power.

So I will make it during these final hours.

I'M JUST A VESSEL and I will never reach perfection,

Until I first learn to be your reflection.

Heavenly Father your goodness endures for all eternity;

In church, on the streets, in heaven and the infirmary.

You created my vessel to contain my soul.

The value of eternity with you is worth more than gold.

Through you Lord Jesus is the only way I can enter,

Because without your grace I will remain a sinner.

I'M JUST A VESSEL and without you there is no me,

But with you I'm a gold vessel that's promised victory.

ETERNAL LIFE

We have ETERNAL LIFE by mercy not by our own works,

So Christianity is more than just going to church.

No matter how righteous the things are we've done,

We can only be saved through Jesus Christ, the Holy One.

The mercy and grace of God and unconditional love,

Constantly descends upon us from heaven above.

Adam first sinned and caused death and mankind's curse,

But Jesus Christ defeated death and gave us a rebirth.

He did this so we can have ETERNAL LIFE and see God's face.

When we accept Jesus as our Savior we are justified by grace.

We are led by the Holy Spirit who pours out truth abundantly

To all of us, not only me.

The definition of Christianity is striving to be like Jesus Christ.

Who came and died for us so we can have

!!! ETERNAL LIFE !!!

<u>MY FATHER</u>

Imagine in the end what would we gain,

If we had everything we wanted but it was all in vain.

What if we had riches, power and tons of success?

If inside ourselves, we were consumed by emptiness?

Money can't buy love, so what can it buy?

Besides we can't take it with us when we die.

It can buy the newest car on the block,

But the car loses its value once it is off the lot.

It can buy us a big home,

But who wants a big house when we're all alone.

MY FATHER has many mansions with streets paved with gold.

And He grants eternal life and peace for our soul.

He'll give us our hearts desire if we're willing to obey,

He'll never lead us wrong; His love is true in every way.

MY FATHER wants you in the family, the choice is yours to make,

I just hope you make up your mind before MY FATHER closes the gate.

ONE OF GOD'S SOLDIERS

I'm one of GOD'S SOLDIERS so the devil will tempt me,

But now that I have God my life's no longer empty.

An idle mind is the devil's playground,

But if I'm too occupied I'd be weighed down.

I'm one of GOD'S SOLDIERS and I'm blessed,

And I will defeat the spirits of worry, fear and stress.

As a soldier I lift up God's holy name.

He helps me stay two steps ahead of the game.

I'm GOD'S SOLDIER so he keeps me safe and provides protection,

And he helps me discern the devils plots of deception.

I'm promised victory when the battles over

Because I'M ONE OF GOD'S SOLDIERS.

TRULY GIFTED

Jesus are the source of life and the master of perfection.

So thank you for saving my soul and giving me direction.

Lord since I found you I feel brand new.

So everything I do I want it to please you.

You've blessed my mind, body, and spirit,

Because of your greatness I'm TRULY GIFTED.

I am highly favored even with my boss.

You watch over me when I'm working and when I'm off.

So wherever I go I proclaim your grace,

On the streets in my home and even the workplace.

You blessed me with a job and the ability to do it well,

And since I'm TRULY GIFTED I will excel.

__TODAY__

TODAY you can be saved from this corrupt generation,

And be able to enjoy the pleasures of having salvation.

You'll be provided confidence in knowing you're saved,

Thanks to Jesus the road has been paved.

TODAY you can experience a joy you've never felt,

The joy of the Lord will make your heart melt.

The more you study, fast and pray,

The easier it will be to listen to God and obey.

When you ask for forgiveness your slate is wiped clean,

And you've secured a position on the winning team.

When you allow God in you'll never be the same,

So God works in ways that can't be explained.

Just a glimpse of Gods power can leave you in awe,

And make TODAY the best day you ever saw.

WE ARE

WE ARE a divine lineage of God's offspring,

So praise to our Father, The King of Kings.

The wise accept our birth right and heed correction,

And believe in the name of Jesus and his resurrection.

WE ARE able to heal the sick and make the blind see.

WE ARE blessed to be part of God's family.

He's the Alpha and Omega beginning and the end,

The only one able to grant repentance and forgiveness for our sins.

We've been giving dominion over wickedness and evil spirits unseen,

God freed us from bondage and all things unclean.

Evil spirits hear the name of Jesus and start shaking,

So God's power goes beyond our imagination.

God tells us He'll never forsake us or leave us on our own.

For WE ARE kingdom children and heirs to his throne.

MY ADDICTION

God I realize it was you I was missing,

While I struggled to overcome MY ADDICTION.

So the message of you sending your Son to die on the cross,

Helps me stay on the path of sobriety without veering off.

No longer am I humiliated by anything I did,

There's also no withdrawal from the high you give.

I never knew the joy of being sober minded,

Because the high from the drugs had me blinded.

I thought I could stop getting high when I wanted but I was wrong,

So I had to humble myself and admit I couldn't do it on my own.

I'm glad wherever I go that you're right there,

With open arms showing me that you care.

So I'm thankful for your grace and I give you praise.

Hallelujah, Amen!!! Your mercy leaves me amazed.

Thank you for looking down from your throne in the sky,

And giving me the strength not to get high.

I anticipate every time your presence descends upon me from above,

Because I'm left with a high that's better than drugs.

Now I can embrace my purpose and fulfill my mission,

Since you saved me and freed me from

!!! MY ADDICTION !!!

A BETTER TOMORROW

It's possible but very hard for a rich man to enter heaven's gates,

Because the love of money can strongly damper one's faith.

It's impossible to serve God when you're focused on cash,

So the desire to get rich can take you extremely fast.

You can be rich, go broke tomorrow,

And be unaware where your cash went.

However, if you put God first you will always be content.

It's true that it's better to give then to receive.

It's true you can have your heart's desire if you pray & believe.

God will bless you with a little today to test your patience and will.

He'll bless you with A BETTER TOMORROW if you're real.

Pay your tithes faithfully and watch what God does,

He'll supply all your needs while surrounding you with his love.

Soon you'll be the lender you won't have to borrow,

Because when you give to God you can expect

!!! A BETTER TOMORROW !!!

GOD'S GLORY

God is my fortress and my shield.

I look at His creation and know He's real.

Jesus is the author and finisher of my faith.

He is my refuge, the one who keeps me safe,

Because there's security and power in His arms.

He's the shelter that keeps me warm.

GOD'S GLORY!!!!

Reveals He's the way, truth and life,

His Word is sharper than a two edge knife.

Everything we need is in God's Word,

So I cast all my worries on the Lord.

He gives me confidence so I don't worry,

Because I'm surrounded by

!!!!! GOD'S GLORY !!!!!

LOVE AND GRACE

When I think of you Lord I give you praise,

Because your LOVE AND GRACE leaves me amazed.

I refer to you as Father or the Great Creator.

Compared to you there is no power greater.

Due to your LOVE AND GRACE you sent Jesus Christ,

And allowed Him to make the ultimate sacrifice.

So you live in my heart and I give you my trust.

I'm a firm believer that not even death will separate us.

Nothing I can do will make me worthy to see your face,

So I'll only be allowed in heaven because you're

!!! LOVE AND GRACE !!!

ALL ABOUT ME

Save ME, guide ME, direct ME,

Forgive ME, strengthen and protect ME.

Shine your light on ME oh Lord.

Let ME gain understanding when I read your Word.

You send people into my life for different reasons,

Some are sent for my lifetime while others just for a season.

So I must be careful how I entertain strangers,

For some are angels sent to warn me of danger.

Others are sent to prepare me for the blessings I'll receive,

To assure ME I'm not forgotten in my time of need.

<u>ONE DAY SOON</u>

ONE DAY SOON Jesus will call us by our names,

And take away all discord, suffering and pain.

We'll go through the divine purpose of transformation

That's been destined since the beginning of creation.

The world will be restored with the wisdom and might of God's Word.

That's the day the Earth will become full of knowledge of the Lord.

ONE DAY SOON every living thing will live in harmony and peace,

From the nursing child to the wildest beast, all violence will cease.

The Son of Righteousness shall arise with healing in his wings,

As Jesus returns ONE DAY SOON and reigns as King.

GOD HAS AN INHERITANCE FOR YOU

If you saw $500.00 on the ground would you keep going? Or
would you claim the cash?
So why not accept the blessings of God instead of letting it pass?
Most people would use cash to provide the things they need.
But the inheritance that God has for you
Guarantees you will succeed.
According to Philippians 4:19 God shall supply
all your needs according to His riches and glory,
Therefore you know you don't have to be worried.
There is freedom in this inheritance,
health, peace, riches and everlasting life.
Even compared to a million dollars I whether have Christ.
Can a million dollars buy you good health or even peace?
Can it separate you from sin as far as the West is from the East?
One thing I know is that money can't get you to paradise,
Because the only way to heaven is through Jesus Christ.
Why not accept the inheritance God gives?
Believe in Jesus and you will live.
The wages of sin is death unless you ask for forgiveness.
Next thing you must do is be about GOD's business.
That means giving God control of your life,
I admit doing right is a fulltime job.
However, there's a priceless inheritance awaiting you
When you become a child of God.

MORE THAN A STATISTIC

I need to slap myself since slavery's been abolished,

And I'm in a penal institute instead of in someone's college.

I enslaved myself while my ancestors were forced,

Should've thought about my legacy while taken an educational course.

There's no denying I'm smart, talented and gifted,

So I find no contentment in being labeled a STATISTIC.

My choices seem to prove the critics correct.

So my insanity is evident and I must need a check.

Living my life in installments may cause me to miss my calling.

If my time in prison was invested into the army I'd be balling.

The army's slogan is "Be all you can be,"

But my current predicament has me listed as a number of D.O.C.

Prisons are full of brothers just like me doing time.

Intelligent young black men who used their smarts for crime.

So as a majority we're labeled STATISTICS

And black balled from jobs,

But I'm MORE THAN A STATISTIC and I will defy the odds.

HOW I LOVE THEE

HOW I LOVE THEE? Let me count the ways,

First off Lord you deserve all the praise.

I'm yours from the bottom to the top,

Therefore, I will worship you until time stops.

I know absence from the body means present with you.

Oh HOW I LOVE THEE and the way you pull me through.

Nobody can compare no matter how hard they try to copy.

You deserve all of me because your love's agape,

In addition, you're so faithful,

This is just one of the reasons I'm so grateful,

Words can't even describe HOW I LOVE THEE.

I know without a doubt, because you have loved me,

through the good, bad and the ugly,

Without trying to judge me.

You have shielded me with your protection and kept me alive,

Without you I honestly wouldn't have survived.

So when I ask the question HOW I LOVE THEE,

The answer will never amount to how much you love me.

MY LETTER TO CHRIST

I start this letter by saying thank you for making me whole by freely giving me a love that's more precious than gold. Before I met you I was out of control and didn't know my role. I was physically enslaved and mentally oppressed. I had one foot in the grave and consumed by stress. I had no reason to strive to stay alive so I found myself wishing to die. Countless nights I cried due to disappointment and numerous lies my struggles seemed magnified. I was angry and bitter inside, on the verge of suicide. Then one day I met you and we slowly began to chill. You were easy to talk to and your compassion was real. I began to reveal my secrets and dreams and the more I opened up the more I healed it seems. You shared words I had never heard. You gave me visions of the life I deserved. This instilled value and took away my shame which allowed me to break free of the bondage of pain. Through you I gained the courage to make a change. Now everybody who knew me tells me I'm not the same. I proclaim the reason I'm even still breathing and no longer a heathen, devoted to cheating, polluting my body with drugs is the same man who took away my hate and replaced it with love. So this letter is to the person who saved my life and welcomed me into the kingdom of light, by paying the ultimate price. So this is My Letter to Jesus Christ.

A LETTER TO THE YOUTH

The Word of God says that we are **WONDERFULLY** and **FEARFULLY** made. So I want to take the time to talk to the youth and tell each and every young person in the world that I think you're all **AWESOME** and **INCREDIBLE.** Each and every one of you have a special talent and gift. You may sing, you may draw, you may write. Actually maybe you have talents other than creative arts. You could be an athlete reading this and then there's a whole lot of other gifts that you may have I haven't mentioned. Instead of one talent, you may have many talents and abilities. One thing that we should all know is that all good things come from GOD. So there is no doubt where your gifts come from.

I also want you to know that we all make mistakes and probably will continue to make mistakes. However we should never allow our mistakes to make us. Neither should we continue to make the same mistake. If you touch a hot stove and it burns you why would you keep touching it? Better yet if I touch a stove and it burns me if I care about you I should try to do what I can to keep you from making the same mistake. I say this to bring up the importance of listening to wisdom and experience.

We can avoid a lot of pain if we just listen to the people who care about us. Sometimes there are things that we are just going to have to learn on our own. There will even be times where we make a mistake we feel like we have to live with it for the rest of our lives. At these times we may feel like we've messed up so much we might as well keep messing up. I tell you right now that is a lie from the devil himself. There is no mistake that is so big that God can't turn around and use for our good.

[ROMANS 8:28 E.S.V.] says "And we know that for those who love God all things work together for good, for those who are called according to his purpose.

So once again you are **WONDERFULLY** and **FEARFULLY** made. There's no mistake big enough that you can make to change this either. Remember that when God says when you ask for forgiveness and ask JESUS into your life we are made new. When we accept Christ in our life we are born again. For a minute I want you to vision a new born baby, all cute and innocent. This is how we start off. But we all know that new born babies make a mess in there pampers. Well just like your parent cleaned up your mess when you were a baby, God will clean up our mess when you are His child. Want to know the best part? When you ask for forgiveness for committing sin He won't ever bring it back up again. He throws it into the sea of forgetfulness and will separate you from as far from that sin as the East is from the West. Can you imagine how far the East is from the West? Imagine riding from New York to California but multiply this by 100 thousand. That's pretty far isn't it?

So as you see once we ask for forgiveness for our mess ups, sins and mistakes they no longer matter to God. So let me ask you a question. What would you do if you saw 500$ laying on the ground and nobody was around? I'm just going to be honest, personally I would first look around and make sure I wasn't being set up. Then I would pick it up and keep it. I say this because God is offering us something a whole lot more than 500$ but there's a whole lot of people walking right past their blessings.

God desires us to be successful. God desires us to have our hearts desires. God wants us to be happy. So I ask you, do you have dreams? God even wants to make those dreams come true. However there are some things we must do. Even if you saw 500$ on the ground, you would have to put some effort into picking it up. It's not going to magically appear in your hand is it? Sometimes we may have to give up people, places, things, and bad habits so that we can live for God and be blessed.

Jesus has done all the hard work already. He defeated the devil so that we can have everlasting life, prosperity, good health, and the fruits of the spirit. Once again though, if we really want to be blessed we must do our part. The truth is GOD HAS AN INHERITANCE WAITING FOR YOU is more than a poem. It's the truth that all of us should receive by faith. The blessings of God are worth more than 500$. They're worth more than even a 1,000,000$. Some people say they just want to be famous. We hear about all kinds of famous people dying every day. The latest was Aretha Franklin who was a very good singer so I mention her name to pay respects. I pray for her soul and keep her family lifted in prayer.

A lot of times we assume that if someone is famous they're automatically rich. There has been other rich and famous people who have committed suicide. Then there are plenty of people who at one time were very rich but died broke and miserable. This is sad but true. This may surprise us but nothing catches God by surprise.

[Mark 8:36] says "What will it profit a man to gain the whole world but forfeit their soul?

Another thing I point out is that we can't buy ourselves into heaven. God says all the gold and silver is his. That's so much gold and silver that the streets of heaven are paved with gold. Can you imagine walking down a street that's made of gold? You'll find out if you live right and remember that you weren't made to fit in and be cool. You will never fit in where you're created to stand out. God says all the cattle on a thousand hills are His. That means he'll shut down Burger King, McDonalds, Wendy's and all the hamburger places if He wanted too. I have nothing against any of these places but my point is everything is truly already God's.

We can't buy ourselves into heaven because eternal life is a free gift that we receive by receiving Jesus. Hopefully you have accepted Jesus as your Lord and Savior but if you haven't done it already, you can do it today. Please don't wait until it's too late.

Some people feel like they're too young to die so they just want to have fun and be cool. How many of you have heard of the rapper Mac Miller, he died on the 9-7-18 due to an suspected overdose reported by Google. He was 26 years old so I pray for the young man's soul and the loss of his family. Due to the world's standard this young man was famous as well as probably rich but it didn't matter.

Too many people use drugs and alcohol thinking they're being cool but sadly to say drugs and alcohol cost them their life. If not their life maybe their freedom. If not their freedom maybe a battle with addiction that costs them their family and keeps them oppressed. If this is cool, why would you want to be cool according to the world's standard anyway?

This reminds me of when I was growing up in Sunday School my grandma Vernell Stidham would always say that cool people end up in one or two places. One is in the grave the other is in prison. I can tell you all about prison but none of it is good. So right now I want you to know once again. You can learn a lot and avoid a lot of pain if you just listen.

We know that the devil comes to steal, kill, and destroy so guess what he's not going to give you anything good. It would be like someone saying they're going pay you for 50$ for working. You know this person is a liar and a thief but you do the work anyways. After you finish working they give you 50$ of monopoly money. How would you feel? You'd probably be upset but why? We all know the devil is the father of lies and we know the wages of sin is death. So either you can allow Jesus to be your Lord and savior or you can live for the devil.

Choose thee, this day who you will serve. Will you accept the inheritance God has for you, or will you remain comfortable living the way you want? Just remember sin is like a jail cell. The devil allows you to be comfortable and you can actually see the door to get out. You think you can get out whenever you want but when you're least expected the cell closes and its count time. Then next thing you know you can't get out the cell. It locks and then the cell turns to hell. I'm praying and pleading that you don't allow this to happen. I'm speaking from a heart of gratefulness because this is exactly what almost happened to me.

I'm only alive today because God is good and the prayers of the righteous availeth much. I'm sure there are people praying for you all and I'm one of them. I hope something I said has gotten your attention. I want you to know that God has an inheritance for you. Also you don't have to be cool by the worlds standard because each of everyone one of you are Wonderfully and Fearfully MADE.

Sincerely,
TyJuan Davis/P.O.E.T.

LETTER TO MY MAMA

Mom you're the type of woman I can always trust, because you will always keep it real and you're so marvelous. Mom you're A QUEEN and you have beauty on the outside with a personality to match. Through the ups and downs of life thanks for standing strong and having my back. Mom you're royal and loyal and always willing to provide support, sometimes even if this means looking beyond your own feelings of disappointments and hurts. You're unselfish but yet don't let the opinions of others control who you are. Therefore you will remain shining as bright as the light of a star. You're a good mother, daughter and a wife. We're all blessed to have you in our life. Mom from now on if I can help it you won't lack a thing because I have realized YOU ARE A QUEEN. So I had to include you in this book a couple of times. This letter was wrote to say "Thank You" and this just a token of my appreciation.

THE TRUEST FORM OF LOVE

THE TRUEST FORM OF LOVE exists regardless and it shines the brightest when time is the darkest. It defies all boundaries. It's natural like the sky the trees, birds, and the bees. It's refreshing like a cool breeze. THE TRUEST FORM OF LOVE looks beyond all situations, death, infidelity and even incarceration. It's present even when you don't love yourself. Even if nobody is offering help, THE TRUEST FORM OF LOVE is standing there with their arms open, holding you together while inside you're truly broken. This form of love is forgiving which means it gladly looks over your inadequacies so you can be happy. They say if you want to know if love is true let it go. However, THE TRUEST FORM OF LOVE is currently washing me whiter then snow.

THIS TYPE OF LOVE

There are many types of love but yours is the greatest of all, because your love will catch me if I were to ever fall. You're more solid then a wall made of concrete, you're the reason why THIS TYPE OF LOVE is so sweet. You're like a pillar of love and support which helps me remain standing on my feet even when it hurts. You are unconditional love and unwavering peace. There is no way THIS TYPE OF LOVE can get truer; you took the place of a thief and a killer. You were accused and abused even though you abided all rules. Laying down your life fulfilled your mission, so that abundant life can be offered to all who listen. THIS TYPE OF LOVE is truly the definition of exemplifying members of opposition. Sadly, it is often thought about when there's a body lying in a coffin. Why, because absence from the body means present with you. Unless the alternative which appears so cruel that it makes some people panic, but like the word says if you love me keep my commandments. We have a choice because love is not forceful instead it's gentle. Though we complicate things more then we should THIS TYPE OF LOVE is simple, because your love is unconditional.

INSPIRATION

If you ask me, "What is your INSPIRATION,"

I'll tell you with no hesitation,

One is all the lonely nights I spent confined.

I was told if you can't do the time

don't do the crime but I did,

So I didn't snitch I just did my bid.

Another INSPIRATION of mine is all the haters,

So called friends who were mostly perpetrators.

I say this because they all abandoned me.

So I thank God for my family.

They were the ones who were there,

To encourage me when I was full of despair.

This book is a token of appreciation

To the haters who filled my heart with motivation.

I'm one with the man that lives within

For He is my guidance and closest friend.

So ask yourself what inspires you to do what you do

I would guess all the things you've been through.

The good, bad and ugly.

My true INSPIRATION comes from knowing God loves me.

GOD'S VOICE

If you want to make sure GOD'S VOICE is heard,

continue to pray and stay in his word.

If you hear GOD'S VOICE you really should obey,

because if not you'll only push God away.

Then the next thing you know you're all alone,

you've back slid and you're living all wrong.

Before that happens take a minute or two,

and hear GOD'S VOICE and what he wants you to do.

God says "acknowledge me and I shall direct your path."

So the devil may laugh, but we'll have the last laugh

God has promised you and me,

that he'll never forsake us and we shall have victory.

Sometimes you may have to bow on your knees,

and go to God with all your cries and pleas.

GOD'S VOICE may be loud and sometimes it may be soft,

but if you listen to GOD'S VOICE you'll never be lost.

TAKEN MY SINS AWAY

I was a blind man walking in the dark,
until God came in and cleansed my heart.
I was falling in a pit that had no bottom,
my life was miserable and filled with problems.
I needed help and I needed it desperately,
I was fighting the devil and he had the best of me.
I was all alone one day when a voice asked loud and clear,
"are you ready for all your sins to disappear?"
At first I thought I had lost my mind,
so I looked all around me three or four times.
When I regained my composure and started to relax,
the same voice came right back.
I didn't know what was going on and I didn't understand it
then the same voice said "calm down don't panic"
the voice said "for a new start all you got to do is repent,
and all your sins will be irrelevant."
At first I was reluctant to believe what I had heard,
but I kept reading and being led by the word.
I was lead to Romans chapter 10 and verse 1,
I was told to believe in the resurrection of his son.
I was so excited by the time I got to verse 10,
I stopped and asked God to forgive me for my sins.
So I got on my knees and I prayed.
When I got up I realized Jesus had taken my sins away.
I was overwhelmed by a supernatural desire,
to run around the room for I felt like I was on fire.
It was no doubt I was saved and would receive the Holy Ghost,
and ever since that day me and God have been close.
For he came in and turned my life around that day,
and that's how I know he has TAKEN MY SINS AWAY.

GOD IS LOVE

GOD IS LOVE and he will keep us safe,

if we follow him and keep the faith.

The Bible says to meditate on God's Word and what it says;

our Father feed 5 thousand with 2 fish and 5 loaves of bread.

The Bible says GOD IS LOVE oh yes it does!!!!!

For He sent his Son to wash us with his blood.

There are many examples of how good God really is.

For Him there's no problem too small nor too big.

GOD IS LOVE and He is the friend of all friends,

He's the alpha and omega – the beginning and the end.

God will not forsake us no matter what we go through

because GOD IS LOVE and He really loves you!!

I CAN DO ALL THINGS

I CAN DO ALL THINGS through Christ which strengthens me!!

For I am no longer in bondage for God has set me free.

God strengthens me every time I read his gospel.

For now I am a child of the kingdom, I am His apostle.

I CAN DO ALL THINGS as God as the head of my life,

for my Father says He will fight my fight.

He's so powerful He says no weapon shall prosper,

and He knows for He is the doctor of all doctors.

I CAN DO ALL THINGS now since I'm one of His children.

I was born again and all my sins are forgiven.

I refuse to go back to the way I was.

For He cleansed my heart and filled it with love.

I CAN DO ALL THINGS now as God directs my steps.

He gave me life and spared me from eternal death.

My God is a good God and I'm blessed to be His,

I CAN DO ALL THINGS for in me He lives.

CLEANSE ME

Lord CLEANSE ME so that I may stand upright,

and be a reflection of your perfect light.

CLEANSE ME from all anger, bitterness, and envy,

so that your light will shine bright in me.

CLEANSE ME so if there is something I should discuss,

I can share your Word righteously and just.

Set my mind on your will and justification,

so I can be a true example of your salvation.

CLEANSE ME so that my hands can plant seeds,

which sprout forth and help others believe.

CLEANSE ME with your Word so that I bring no shame.

Teach me how to free others from their pain.

CLEANSE ME so I recognize your voice and obey, so that you

can use me as a living testimony in Jesus name I pray.

GOD THE ALMIGHTY

GOD THE ALMIGHTY is the King of Kings!!!
There's no doubt, He's the Lord of the rings.
With Him in control we will not fail,
with His loving grace we can bypass the fire of hell.
Through GOD THE ALMIGHTY we can do it all,
if we keep the faith we will continue to stand tall.
We are promised victory from the start,
if we can just keep His commandments in our hearts.
GOD THE ALMIGHTY declares that He will not forsake us,
so if we stand on God's Word the devil can't overtake us.
Even if our spirits are broken as long as we don't doubt,
GOD THE ALMIGHTY will work everything out.

WE REAP WHAT WE SOW

WE REAP WHAT WE SOW, so we sow what we reap.

So we should be careful what we do and how we speak.

Be cautious not to make others stumble,

and never allow pride to stop you from being humble.

God says "those who are weak will be made strong"

"and those who are faithful will make heaven their home."

God says "I'll forgive you, how you forgive others"

So we'll be treated the way we treat our brothers.

So hold on to this fact and don't let go,

and make sure you remember WE REAP WHAT WE SOW.

When we come to God praying about our situation,

we should call out in faith instead of desperation.

We should use all of our senses especially our eyes,

so that we may walk the walk and stay focused on the prize.

I look back at my life and see how much I've changed,

and I truly understand why if there's no pain there's no gain.

I was once caught in a trap and living a lie,

now I'm standing on the truth. I'm saved and sanctified.

So I have faith that I will continue to grow,

and I'm careful how I treat others,

!! WE REAP WHAT WE SOW !!

I'M SAVED

I come to you in faith instead of desperation,

because you Lord can exceed all my expectations.

Since I'M SAVED I know I'm not alone,

for your presence descends on me from your throne.

You may not come when I want you to,

but I know, that you Lord will get me through.

At one time I just existed, I wasn't even living,

now I'M SAVED and my sins are forgiven.

I'll never forget the day I was reborn,

that was the day my whole life was transformed.

I'M SAVED and I submit to your Holy voice,

I think about your love for me and I begin to rejoice.

I was a prisoner of sin and my life was almost done,

but now I'M SAVED because of your Holy Son.

Thank you for your love and delivery,

and the faith to know that you hear me.

You will answer my cries and my pleas when I pray,

and all you ask is that I obey.

There were two thieves by your side on the cross,

and the one that accepted you was not lost.

Now that I'M SAVED I have faith,

that I also will enter heaven's gates.

I PRAY

First thing I do in the morning is take time and I PRAY,

Lord please give me the spiritual nourishment I need today.

Throughout the day give me strength to endure,

and the peace of mind to keep my heart pure.

When I feel the devil attacking, I take a time-out,

and I PRAY that you Lord keep me just and devout.

I will not allow myself to lose focus of the prize,

because if I take my eyes off of you I won't survive.

The Bible says you'll never forsake me, no not ever,

so I trust in you Lord and believe we're always together.

I was once like the guy in the story of the footprints,

because when I saw one set, I'd wonder where you went.

Now I know at my lowest points you carry me in your arms,

you are my fortress in the middle of the storm.

So Lord as I go through my day and journey along this path,

I PRAY for strength and endurance that my salvation will last.

THE GOOD NEWS

Lord you gave me the gift of writing,

So Lord I hope others find your GOOD NEWS exciting.

I am really just a vessel, Lord these are your words,

I am just sharing THE GOOD NEWS of the God I serve.

You are the living God worthy of all praise,

So I'll give you the honor for the rest of my days.

Through telling others of your GOOD NEWS,

I'm rebuking the devil and giving him the blues.

Lord I humble myself and draw nearer,

For as I read my Bible THE GOOD NEWS becomes clearer.

If I can touch one life with the talent you've given me,

I have no doubt we'll both be held within your security.

Lord you are my protection and my shield.

So I take your GOOD NEWS with me out in the battlefield.

It is a spiritual battle all around us,

But we'll win if we give you our trust.

I'm going to keep writing because it produces strength,

For it is not flesh and blood we wrestle against

But evil spirits and wickedness that is unseen.

So Lord I pray that you keep my spirit clean,

And keep revealing THE GOOD NEWS you want me to share.

So that when the devil attacks I'll be prepared.

GIVE HIM PRAISE

God created us to GIVE HIM PRAISE,

so let's GIVE HIM PRAISE until the end of our days.

When praises go up blessings come down.

The God we serve sits in heaven with the stars as His crown.

Jesus is the King of Kings!!!!!

Let's praise Him with the songs we sing.

I GIVE HIM PRAISE in the poems I write

for He is the way, the truth, and the life.

Our Father shines in the darkest dark

therefore let's GIVE HIM PRAISE with all of our hearts.

Let's GIVE HIM PRAISE with our hands,

even in circumstances we don't understand.

God is the Creator of all.

If we keep him first we will not fall.

The devil is busy trying to get our attention,

for he doesn't want us to complete our mission.

The devil wants to be a hindrance and a thorn in our side,

but he will not succeed no matter how hard he tries.

As long as we continue to serve God and

!!! GIVE HIM PRAISE. !!!

<u>YOU ARE</u>

I focus on you and keep my eyes on the prize,

for Jesus YOU ARE my strength and my will to survive.

YOU ARE the air in my lungs, the breath of all life,

YOU ARE joy and happiness without worry and strife.

YOU ARE my peace of mind in the midst of a violent storm,

for I know you will protect me and keep me unharmed.

Jesus YOU ARE good and everything good comes through you.

With you there is nothing I can't do.

YOU ARE love and your love is sweet.

You give me confidence when otherwise I'd be weak.

There's really no words to describe how good YOU ARE.

You're so amazing your birth was marked by the north star.

I don't know how mankind could deserve your loving grace,

but I hope one day I see your face.

Jesus YOU ARE closer than any brother or friend

so on judgment day I hope YOU ARE the one to let me in.

HAVE YOUR WAY

God I look back and see how far I've come,

since I gave you my life and allowed your will to be done.

I'm still not where I should be but I'm farther than I was,

due to your grace and everlasting love.

I know I still have a long way to travel

for I'm engaged in an ongoing battle.

HAVE YOUR WAY with me as I strive to live right.

Give me the strength so that I may serve Jesus Christ.

Lord you are my strength when I am weak.

So keep my soul at night when I sleep.

Every day I'm striving to keep on the path that's straight

by staying in my Word and keeping the faith.

Lord you are the potter and I am the clay

so continue to mold me and

!!!! HAVE YOUR WAY !!!!

SURROUND ME WITH YOUR LOVE

I sit here and think of your loving grace o' Lord,

and I'm drawn to reflect and write in regards to your Word.

I feel like lately I've been falling short of your glory

and Lord I can't lie I'm a little worried.

I know you said we should not worry or fear

but I need to know my prayers aren't falling on deaf ears.

Lord I'm nothing without you, without you I would not be.

I was once chained by sins but you set me free.

I know the devil comes to steal, kill, and destroy,

and you came to give life and unspeakable joy.

The world didn't give me my joy so they can't take it away.

Lord I want to see your face when it's judgment day.

I don't want to be like the Pharisees and just put on a show.

Instead I want to be filled with the Holy Spirit from head to toe.

Lord I don't care what men do, who are they to judge?

Lord I just want you to

!! SURROUND ME WITH YOUR LOVE !!

AS I FOLLOW YOU

Lord AS I FOLLOW YOU and proceed,

give me the strength and wisdom that I need.

As I go forward in my journey as you as my guide,

give me the spirit of discernment as I decide,

to put one foot in front of the other AS I FOLLOW YOU.

Lord bless me to understand what you want me to do.

Your Word clearly tells me to not lean on my own insight,

for sometimes I may be wrong but you are always right.

You are perfect and you make no mistakes.

AS I FOLLOW YOU and take the path you have me to take,

you'll order my steps so that I will know my role.

Lord right now I surrender to you and give you complete control.

Lord AS I FOLLOW YOU give me knowledge and courage.

Knowledge to know your voice and courage to not ignore it.

When I was young I didn't listen or heed to correction,

but now AS I FOLLOW YOU, you provide me direction.

I have now realized you're all I need and much more,

so bless me AS I FOLLOW YOU and go forth.

THANKS TO JESUS

I give THANKS TO JESUS for dying on the cross,

so that my sins would be forgiven and I won't be lost.

You're the manifestation of holy perfection

so "Thank You" for displaying your power by your resurrection.

I give THANKS TO JESUS for He is our mediator,

to God the Father the Great Creator.

Jesus is the way, the truth, and the life.

The only way to be saved is through Jesus Christ

THANKS TO JESUS for coming upon Earth and saving us all,

but it's up to each of us individually to answer His call.

Some of us are called to be prophets others are preachers,

some are called to be deacons while others are teachers.

We all are connected for the greater purpose of praise,

so let's fight the good fight until the end of our days.

"The battle is not yours" says the Lord.

That's why it's very important we have faith in the God's Word.

Jesus came and conquered sickness, sin, and temptation.

THANKS TO JESUS we can have salvation.

WE HAVE A MISSION TO COMPLETE

We prosper through God's love and our faith.

The devil wreaks havoc with weapons like deceit and hate.

The devil is a master of casting illusions,

and that's why he's known as the author of confusion.

God desires for us to see through the devil's trickery.

This is why God has promised us eternal victory.

We know God does not lie and He does not fail.

So why would we even question if we will prevail?

We need to recognize that the devil is full of hate & deceit,

and no matter what he does, he is destined to defeat.

Remember that we do not wrestle against flesh and blood.

So continue to be a living example of God's love.

Regardless of what the devil tries to do to make us weak,

we as children of God

!! HAVE A MISSION TO COMPLETE !!

I REMEMBER

Lord right now I want to give you thanks for I REMEMBER,
when my soul was lost and I was a sinner.
When you forgave me for all of the sins I've committed
I was reborn and ever since then my life has been different.
I REMEMBER chasing women looking for love.
I was looking for God and didn't know I was.
I was a menace to society, selling drugs in my community.
Now I go through my hood telling of how God set me free.
I REMEMBER throwing up gang signs wearing orange and blue
now I throw up my hands and give praise to you.
I REMEMBER I used to hope I didn't get caught selling dope,
now I realize without you I have no hope.
I REMEMBER all the times I disappointed my mother,
now I have you and you're closer than any brother.
I was close to the edge surely living my life in vain,
now I've found my purpose in praising your Holy name.
I REMEMBER set tripping with my rivals,
now I have peace when I read my Bible.
So even though right now I'm in a jail cell,
I want to thank you that I'm not burning in hell.
Sadly everyday somebody dies and a soul is lost,
even though you sent your Son to die on the cross.
Every day I REMEMBER what you've done for me,
and I REMEMBER the day you set me free.

STRONGER THAN I'VE EVER BEEN

Since I'm no longer controlled by my flesh,

my life has been prosperous and I've been blessed.

I still have tribulations and trials,

but my faith in the Lord helps me to smile.

Now that I've allowed Jesus to come in,

I'm STRONGER THAN I'VE EVER BEEN.

I know God loves me for the Bible tells me so.

Therefore I place in the Lord my trust and confidence,

no matter what the devil does or what I go against.

I am a child of the kingdom and I'm promised victory,

for wherever I am the Lord is with me.

I constantly strive to be a reflection of God's light,

therefore He guides me and keeps me living right.

Ever since God freed me from my sins, I'm

!! STRONGER THAN I'VE EVER BEEN !!

<u>HAVE YOUR WAY</u>

God I look back and see how far I've come,

since I gave you my life and allowed your will to be done.

I'm still not where I should be but I'm farther than I was,

due to your grace and everlasting love.

I know I still have a long way to travel,

for I'm engaged in an ongoing battle.

HAVE YOUR WAY with me as I strive to live right.

Give me the strength so that I may serve Jesus Christ.

Lord you are my strength when I am weak.

Keep my soul when I sleep!!!

Every day I strive to keep walking straight,

by staying in your Word and keeping the faith.

Lord you are the potter and I am the clay.

Continue to mold me and

!!!! HAVE YOUR WAY !!!!

BRIGHTEN MY WAY

Lord give me the strength to be a laborer of your harvest.

Especially at times when the horizon is the darkest.

You don't need any fair weathered guys.

You need those who are filled and sanctified.

Use my weaknesses to make me see clearly.

Use my strengths to draw others near me.

BRIGHTEN MY WAY and clear my path,

guide me so that I can complete my tasks.

Put a hedge around your people,

so that they will not become overtaken by evil.

Give me enthusiasm when it comes to your will.

So that your light will constantly be revealed.

Just as the sun is our natural light during the day,

allow me to use your Word to

!!!!! BRIGHTEN MY WAY !!!!!

CLOSER TO

Sometimes our situation,

may not match our revelation.

However we must continue to stay strong.

As we grow CLOSER TO God and hold on,

our faith will grow like a seed.

Doors will open and reveal everything we need.

God is the same yesterday, today, and tomorrow.

Fear not for He didn't give us the spirit of sorrow.

As we grow CLOSER TO God we'll release all worry.

The God we serve is a God of glory.

We were in bondage but now we're set free

He washed us with the blood and freed us from captivity.

Let's keep God's Word and stand firm!!!!!!

We are His children and we shall not be harmed.

Trials can draw us CLOSER TO God and strengthen our souls.

Remember fire takes the impurities out of gold.

Don't get discouraged when things don't go right.

This is the time we grow CLOSER TO Jesus Christ.

IT'S ALL UP TO YOU

God says none of our needs will be neglected.

So no problem in life is big enough to offset it.

IT'S ALL UP TO YOU if you're blessed or cursed.

Line your ways up with God and put him first.

Let God be in control and watch what happens.

Your faith will put the Word of God into action.

Jesus spoke miracles and we can do the same.

If your faith is hindering you, who can you blame?

Just compare where you are now to where you were.

You'll see God's power is hard to ignore.

Remember when your head was down and you was depressed.

Now look you're full of joy and your life is blessed.

The Word says It's better to give then to receive,

so you should know that God will supply your needs.

Give thanks to God to whom credit is due

& remember God gave you the power, so

!!!! IT'S ALL UP TO YOU !!!!

YOUR WILL BE DONE

Dear God I call upon your holy name,

and pray you send down your latter rain.

When praises go up blessings come down.

I was lost until Jesus came, and now I'm found.

God you are good and you are great.

Lord you are perfect you make no mistakes.

I pray for the strength to resist the desires of my flesh.

I pray I am where I need to be so I am blessed.

Open my ears so I can hear you loud and clear.

Cleanse my heart and take away all failure and fear.

Touch my mind so I can understand your will.

Open my eyes so your plan for my life will be revealed.

Lord thank you for giving your only begotten Son

Lord I pray !! YOUR WILL BE DONE !!!!

DO FOR YOU

There is no secret what God can DO FOR YOU.

Just as He's blessed others, He'll bless you too.

This is why He wants us to share our personal stories.

We have the testimonies to show God's glory.

God gives us strength, multiplies, heals, and medicates,

even allows us to move mountains with our faith.

Jesus freed us from the bondage of our sinful flesh.

Come to Him if you're heavy laden, He'll give you rest.

These are just a few of the many things God does.

He is the definition of unconditional love.

He'll make you a new being and do away with the old.

Eternal life can be yours if you give God control.

I can go on and on about what God can do but

You won't know unless you let God

!!!! DO FOR YOU !!!!

POWER OVER MY ENEMIES

Yeah devil I hear you calling my name,

but I know you have already been slain.

My Father took away all my iniquities.

Gives me POWER OVER MY ENEMIES.

We wrestle not against flesh and blood.

Divided we fall but together we stand in love.

In the name of Jesus I will not allow you to make me weak.

Get thee behind me Satan for you are full of deceit.

God gives me POWER OVER MY ENEMIES so I can survive.

I tell you devil, you can run but you can't hide.

Jesus came into the world and took away my transgressions.

In exchange He gave me eternal life as a prized possession.

My Father's in heaven with streets paved with gold.

So what would it benefit me to gain the world and lose my soul?

No matter the temptations and earthly afflictions,

I'll keep going until I complete my mission.

I know that I have been promised the victory

and God gave me

!! POWER OVER MY ENEMIES !!

LIVE AGAIN

Death reigned from Adam to Moses in men alike.

Mankind was given a second chance through Jesus Christ.

Many deaths reigned by the offense of one.

Even more will be saved by the grace of God's Son.

When we were sinners, Jesus died on the cross.

Surely when we get saved we will not be lost.

Through Jesus we receive reconciliation.

Let's share this good news throughout the entire nation.

Where sin reigned in death, grace reigns more than ever before.

So we don't have to be punished for Adam's sin anymore.

Jesus came into the world and died for our sins.

Thanks to Jesus we can all

!!!! LIVE AGAIN !!!!

EXAMPLE AFTER EXAMPLE

Time after time and EXAMPLE AFTER EXAMPLE.

We're shown there's nothing God can't handle.

Do you remember how Daniel was protected in the lion's den?

How about how the Israelites were freed from the Egyptians?

Consider Jonah in the belly of the whale.

What about Peter in the jail cell.

Joseph rose to a ruler after being a slave.

God raised Jesus from the grave.

Job lost all and regained all his possessions and kids.

How could we ever forget all the things Jesus did?

After all these things why do we doubt and stray?

When we know that we'll face God one day.

We can move a mountain with the faith the size of a seed.

So it's clear if we believe we can receive.

When you feel yourself doubting please begin to pray.

Don't stop praying until that doubt goes away.

Pull out your Bible where's it's
EXAMPLE AFTER EXAMPLE.

Of God's power and you'll see there's nothing God can't handle.

GIVE GOD YOUR TRUST

If you keep the faith you will receive,

so GIVE GOD YOUR TRUST & get everything you need.

Why should you give the devil power over your life?

The only way to heaven is through Jesus Christ

Do not all sinners go to hell and lose their soul?

So why would you not let God keep you whole?

I'm just asking about your beliefs and opinions.

It's not us but the God in us with the power and dominion.

God never changes and He'll do for all.

He healed the sick and made the cripple stand tall.

GIVE GOD YOUR TRUST and you'll realize He's real.

!!! **By His stripes we are healed** !!!

Whatever problem you face He will solve for you.

GIVE GOD YOUR TRUST and let Him do what He can do.

He gave us free will and left the choices up to us.

It's up to us to decide to

!!!! GIVE GOD YOUR TRUST !!!!

GOD GAVE ME

GOD GAVE ME a special task to perform.

So I pray that I'm ready when it's my turn.

GOD GAVE ME special talents to share with others.

I plan can to be a light to my sisters and brothers.

GOD GAVE ME this message of encouragement and support,

to let you know God doesn't want you to hurt.

I wrote these poems to lighten your load.

Also I want to reassure you God is in control.

Sometimes life is hard and it can drive you insane.

It's not God's desire for you to feel pain.

Everything good comes from above,

because God is good and God is love.

If these words GOD GAVE ME sounds like a sweet tune,

it's because God wants you to know

your troubles will be over soon.

GOD'S LOVE

I journey down this lonely road for I'm in pursuit

of GOD'S LOVE for it will reveal the truth.

My whole body is full of the fervent desire

to fulfill my Father's purpose no matter what it requires.

Only GOD'S LOVE will make me whole

for what will I gain if I lost my soul.

Every day I seek GOD'S LOVE and deliverance,

and I pray He removes all hindrances.

I've experienced what I thought was love but it was vain

but since then I've realized all love is not the same.

There's sexual lust and love for significant others,

there's love for your mom, dad, sisters, and brothers.

Then there is love for friends.

GOD'S LOVE never ends.

It's everlasting and unselfish, and it's from above,

this love is agape and it's the most profound type of love.

This love even allows someone to love their enemies,

such as when we were sinners and GOD'S LOVE sat us free.

We were ensnared with transgressions and we lost, until

GOD'S LOVE sent His only begotten son to die on the cross

NOTHING BUT A DREAM

It's true in order to receive, you must believe

And if you're lazy nothing will ever be achieved.

You can have the biggest hopes and dreams

But something's aren't as easy as they seem.

However, you'll never know if you always quit

Since what you put in, is exactly what you're going to get.

It's okay to dream, but it's what you do that matters

But as you get older and time goes faster,

You'll begin to see that the longer you procrastinate,

Is the more time you waste.

My advice to you is to go after whatever it is

Because you and I only get one life to live.

So remember that you can have your heart's desires

But only if you're willing to do what it requires.

You can have the plans and answers for everything

But until you make it happen its

!!!!! NOTHING BUT A DREAM !!!!!

WHO I AM

Here lately I've been the source of a lot of hate

So I decided to take the time and set the record straight.

It's unbelievable all the negativity I have received.

Are people mad because they didn't think I'd succeed?

I'm a man who was down but I wasn't out,

so I ended up in prison and took another route.

Wasn't I supposed to change,

when I learned that life wasn't a game?

Yeah I was banged out and yeah I was tripping,

but I matured and became a different man in prison.

I learned what life is and now see the whole picture

I look outside the box and began to dream bigger.

So I'll let you'll keep comparing statistics,

because WHO I AM is a man that is very gifted.

I'm my own man and soon to be entrepreneur,

while I was gone I became wiser and more mature.

They say a person's is only as good as their word.

So you would know WHO I AM if you listen and observe.

AS I GET OLDER

AS I GET OLDER the more I realize I don't know.

And ironically the faster time seems to go.

I'm 29 right now by the time I'm a free man I'll be 30

I remember when I was a kid trying not to get dirty.

Now I'm a grown man trying to dodge the penitentiary

My little brothers have graduated with college degrees.

AS I GET OLDER the more my bones seem to ache,

it also seems like I've gained some unwanted weight.

I used to stay up playing video games all night.

Now I stay up praying and serving Jesus Christ.

When I was young I couldn't wait to get grown.

now I see it's no fun paying bills on my own.

I'm at the age all my friends have sons and daughters

but me I'm still questioning am I to be a father.

Lord knows I want a kid or two.

For I no longer look at life like I used too.

Before I die I want to pass on my name

As I've gotten older my whole life has changed.

I realize I don't want to come back to prison.

AS I GET OLDER the more I realize why I'm living.

MY DIVINE PURPOSE

I can't reach MY DIVINE PURPOSE,

until I go through the stages of metamorphous.

So until then I slowly creep around

crawling on my stomach pacing the ground.

I'm anxious to trade this shell for wings so bright,

but I can't fulfill my potential until the time is right.

So I stay patient and wait,

for my life to reshape.

It's going to be like a resurrection,

because I must go to sleep to reach perfection.

If you don't see me, don't fill with concern,

just trust that I have been transformed.

When I come back out of my core,

I will not be as I was before.

So don't allow my absence to bring you any pain,

instead be happy for my goal has been obtained.

Instead of crawling I'm now able to fly

for I have reached MY DIVINE PURPOSE of being a butterfly.

MONOPOLY AND LIFE

Have you ever played MONOPOLY to past the time?
It caused time to pass and helped you relax your mind.
You went around the board and won a lot of money,
brought property, went to jail and thought it was funny
You landed on others properties and had to pay rent.
You looked at the clock and wondered where time went.

Life sometimes reminds me of a game of MONOPOLY.
I was trying to win while others tried to stop me.
I rolled the dice and ended up losing a turn,
For now, I'm in jail with a lesson to learn.
In life there's people as real as that colored paper.
They may be real, yeah some real haters.
They're always hating and trying to bring you pain
so remember life is not a game.

You may buy property and accumulate revenue,
But you can't start over when you want to.
So look at life and whatever you do monopolize,
Take your time to plan and strategize.
Because when you realize I'm right
You'll see the similarities and differences of
!!!! MONOPOLY AND LIFE !!!!

GENOCIDE

If we come together we can conquer all,
because united we stand and divided we fall.
That's why the white man supplies drugs and guns
for why educate a man when you can keep him dumb?
A GENOCIDE is occurring due to our own hands.
We're doing a better job than the Ku Klux Klan.
Since the beginning oppression has been upon our heads
that's why so much blood and tears have been shed.
We must defeat this GENOCIDE or remain impoverished
for we are free since slavery is abolished.
But it won't matter if you're enslaved in your own mind
why do you think it's so many blacks doing time?
If you limit yourself who can you blame?
No one, because you're responsible for your own change.
Martin Luther King Jr. died for his dream.
Yet we haven't realized that we are truly kings.
Until we put everything else aside.
we'll keep dying off and causing our own
!!!!!! GENOCIDE !!!!!!

THE NEXT GENERATION

I have concern for THE NEXT GENERATION
For there's a major crisis throughout this nation.
It seems as though earth has been cursed.
Every generation seems to get worse.

This madness has been occurring for quite a while.
It's sad for it takes a village to raise a child.
Due to incarceration the village is deteriorating,
It's as though all values and morals are quickly fading.

A lot of fathers are in prison.
We're having to lean more on our women.
Truth be told, they can only do so much.
For even putting food on the table can be tough.
They're doing all they can.
But a woman can't teach a boy how to be a man.

THE NEXT GENERATION is growing up gang-banging.
Stealing, killing, and dope-slanging.
They're lucky to have a father figure
Most are forced to grow up quicker.
Therefore, kids are having kids.
Sad to say but it's the way it is.
It's up to us as adults to fix the situation.
Let's pray, set an example, and support
!!!!!! THE NEXT GENERATION !!!!!!

I'M JUST A BABY

People think I can't talk but maybe it's they don't listen.

I'll tell you what I want if you only pay attention.

I can't lie I'm a little selfish, so it's all about me.

Can you imagine 9 months in a woman's tummy?

Why is it when I'm hungry you think I'm sleepy?

When I need a new diaper you try to feed me?

You're always making funny noises and making me scared.

Then you wonder why I cry and try to pull your hair.

I'M JUST A BABY so yeah I have a little stomach.

If you feed me too much I will vomit.

I learn how to talk by listening to what you say.

I learn how to crawl because I'm trying to get away.

When crawling doesn't work I learn how to walk.

I think maybe if I learn how to run I won't get caught!

God says you can learn something from me,

But that probably won't happen because

!!! I'M JUST A BABY !!!

MINI ME

God blessed me when he gave me a baby boy.

For he's a MINI ME, my little bundle of joy!

When I look at him he reminds me.

How truly wonderful it is to have a family.

I want him to have the things I never had.

It is my responsibility to be a good dad.

A lot of men don't get the privilege to bear a seed.

So I'll do everything I can to see my son succeed.

For he's a MINI ME from my looks to personality.

When he was born my dream became a reality.

So I hope one day I can explain and let him know.

Why I call him MINI ME and love him so!

WHAT IS LOVE?

WHAT IS LOVE? Love is Jesus ascending from above.

Love is longsuffering and doesn't keep track,

Because love conquers all and that's a fact.

Love is trustworthy and honest.

Love will make you keep a promise.

Love is complete in its course.

Love is without pressure and without force.

Love is special in the way it unites.

Love brings fulfillment and delight.

WHAT IS LOVE?

Love is a treasure that can't be measured.

Love is a very enjoyable pleasure.

Love is sacrificial and dedicated.

Love is not only talked about but also demonstrated.

Love endures through all situations.

Love goes beyond the barriers of incarceration.

Love will bridge over others inadequacies.

Love will encourage you and keep you happy.

Love is the truth even when it hurts.

True love does not deceive but instead it comforts.

Love does not neglect,

Instead it's a constant source of support and respect.

There are five types of love but my love is simple,

For the love I have for you is unconditional.

FOREVER A QUEEN

If there was no you there would be no us,

Though woman came from our ribs and we came from the dust.

You'll are the carriers of the next generation,

And when a baby arrives you'll are the ones stuck in the situation.

You'll could have an abortion but a baby is a living person,

And in the end you'll are the ones left hurting.

So being a woman can sometimes be an unfair job,

But you'll are created the way you are by God.

So I respect you and the things you go through,

You're FOREVER A QUEEN but how you act is up to you.

Behind every strong man is a strong female,

Because you are the strength when we may fail.

If I'm saying something new to your ears it's a shame,

Because a woman's worth, will and has never changed.

In a lot of ways, you are our everything,

And that's why a woman will be

!!!! FOREVER A QUEEN !!!!

A HOUSE IS NOT A HOME

Papa was a rolling stone,

only because he didn't know A HOUSE IS NOT A HOME.

Well a lot of people think a house is a home but it isn't.

Listen to me and I'll tell you the difference.

A house is just a place to live,

while a home is where your heart is.

A home is full of joy, excitement, and support,

for it takes two to make a home what it's worth.

That's why I'm lucky to have the wife I have.

After a long day I can look forward to a bubble bath.

I can also anticipate a hot meal to eat,

since I'm married I no longer need to run the streets.

At home I got a beautiful wife, she's my best friend,

now when I'm out and about I'm anxious to get back in.

For everything I want is at home waiting on me,

if I lived alone I could never be so happy.

Before we met my home was just a house,

for I never knew what companionship was about.

Now I feel loved instead of feeling alone,

and that's why

!! A HOUSE IS NOT A HOME !!

DEEPER THAN US

Baby I'm a man now, I'm no longer a boy,

So I realize your heart is not a toy.

Our relationship has become DEEPER THAN US,

Because I've given God all our problems and all my trust.

Through time and tribulations, I have changed,

Since I'm living for God I'm not the same.

I prayed to God and He answered my call,

So I'm obligated to give my all.

I know you've been hurt and are reluctant to give in,

But I promise to never hurt you again.

I made a vow to you and the man upstairs,

He knows my heart and how much I care.

Trust in God and He will give us strength to hold on,

For this is DEEPER THAN US and we are not alone.

You may not know how deep my love is for you,

But God knows my love is true.

THE SOUND OF QUIETNESS

THE SOUND OF QUIETNESS occurs when everything is quiet,

It can make you calm even when you're feeling violent.

it can help you gather thoughts and regain control.

THE SOUND OF QUIETNESS is even good for your soul.

When your life is chaotic and filled with confusion,

within THE SOUND OF QUIETNESS may lay the solution.

it will help you concentrate on what the problem is,

with a positive outlook on life nothing seems to big.

THE SOUND OF QUIETNESS supplies you a peace of mind,

A sense of relief that you wish could last a lifetime.

THE SOUND OF QUIETNESS is a help when you meditate,

it gives you the time to think before you make a mistake.

it will help you relax when you are sore,

It's nothing like it in the midst of an uproar.

its keen to the relationship with you and the Lord,

for you are able to hear his voice and heed God's Word.

THE SOUND OF QUIETNESS appears when everything is still,

within THE SOUND OF QUIETNESS true joy can be fulfilled.

ALL I CAN

Instead of playing games,

you should be reassuring me that you feel my pain.

It seems like you're playing with me like I'm a fool,

and baby that really isn't cool.

I'm already in a cold situation as it is,

it hurts to be away from you and my kids.

All I ask is that you continue to hold it together,

because baby I'm not going to be in prison forever.

Is it too much to ask you to keep it real?

I've never left unsure about how I feel.

I just need you to understand,

that I'm giving 100% and doing ALL I CAN.

I can't do much in this situation but I'm doing my part,

but that doesn't mean you can play with my heart.

We should not play with each other's emotions.

I've never been one for empty wishing and hoping,

so I'm doing ALL I CAN for you.

I'm always going to keep it real and you should too.

Two can play games but why take that risk?

So I'm doing ALL I CAN to keep the games out of this.

THIS BOOK

Some might read THIS BOOK,
others may not even take a second look,
but this was something I did for me,
God, my supporters, and my family.
I thought about it and decided I would try
To come up with a way never to die.
So if I sell one copy or many more
I believe THIS BOOK will open many doors.
I've had this talent all along
But always had too many other things going on.
So maybe God needed to get my attention
And that's why he allowed me to go to prison.
While I was in there I learned a lot
Especially the times spent on 23hr lock.
However, those were the times that strengthened me
Spiritually, physically, and mentally.
I stayed praying to God for things to go well
Hoping to make it home and to stay out of jail.
So I spent a lot of time writing and just trying to chill
I got in touch with myself and began to heal.
In the process THIS BOOK was conceived
But nothing in life is guaranteed.
So if This Book sells a million copies
Or if writing just remains one of my hobbies.
I've found out that once I begin to write
And paper and pen ignite,
I'm capable of writing about anything
Because I've been in most of the situations life can bring.
But I've made the best of it
So THIS BOOK is my testament.

AFTERWORD

It's a blessing to have life and the opportunity another day presents. Now that I have given my life to Christ and my mind is being renewed. A lot of times we read scriptures that emphasis what Jesus' Resurrection means to us however until we experience a true manifestation of God's power we will not understand what Jesus' Resurrection truly means. I am encouraged and I find hope in the fact that a true change has begun in me. I can sincerely say that no matter what our past looks like when we are allow Jesus into our life we are made a new creation. Doesn't mean that things will all of a sudden things will become perfect. We will still endure tests and hardships but truthfully it can be these very same uncomfortable and trying circumstances we need to encounter to bring us closer to God.

In our Saviors case it was three days in the grave. In Jonah's case it was three days in the belly of the whale In my case it was not one but three trips to prison. As a former three time felon, I can understand how a lot of people who go to prison find themselves lost and without hope. So they get out and go back to what they know. This is sad because prison is basically one step from the grave. Why do you think a jail cell and a coffin is almost the same size??... With 70% of the people I interacted with on a daily basis having a life sentence. I can personally understand in [Psalms 23:4] when David said "Though I walk through the valley of the shadow of death, I will fear no evil, for you are with me, your rod and staff comfort me."

I'm sure you've heard three strikes and you're out but I TELL YOU SOMETHING. God's rod and staff comforted me and the very thing that the devil intended to use to destroy me is the very same thing that God used for my good.

This is why it's important to renew our mind daily. When I came out of prison I wasn't only a free man but I was a new man. Statistically the first year after a person regains their freedom is the hardest. Change is a process and it doesn't happen overnight.

[ROMANS 12:2 AMP] says Do not be conformed to this world [any longer with it's superficial values and customs], but be transformed and progressively changed [as you mature spiritually] by the renewing of your mind [focusing on godly values and ethical attitudes], so that you may prove [for yourselves] what the will of God is, that which is good and acceptable perfect [in his plan and purpose for you]

Now that I'm saved and I'm healthier, and happier. A true Change Within Me has taken place. The more I devote myself to God the more renewed my mind becomes. God saved me and this shows he can save anybody. God can not only break the yoke of bondage, He can obliterate the yoke and cleans up the mess without leaving one trace of residue.

Quite a few people saw Jesus being crucified on the cross. However when they went to go look for Jesus in the grave He was gone. They looked around they don't see his body. This is encouraging to hold on to and I'll tell you why.

A lot of times people won't be able to believe their eyes when we testify about what we've been through or what God has done for us. It's hard for the human mind to grasp the supernatural. It's hard to believe the last time you saw someone they were dead now they're alive. They were blind but now they see. They we're crippled now they're walking. The yoke of sin which can so easily entangle us have not only been broke but has been obliterated and there is no evidence of what was before.

This also why it's not only important but crucial we allow The Word of God to transform us. When we do we can trust it's only going to empower us. We must receive it by faith.

In a world where a lot of people want the benefits but not many are willing to put forth effort we're often influenced by what we see and think. However once we realize half the battle is in our minds life will become easier. Our attitudes will change. Our focus will change and a true change will occur. Besides the battle don't belong to us. Instead it belongs to the Lord. The beginning of knowledge begins with the fear of the Lord. After this a true Change can and will take place.

ABOUT THE AUTHOR

TyJuan Davis is my name, me and most men are not the same.

Though I will never claim to be better than the rest,

I'm a man of God, so I'm not controlled by my flesh.

I enjoy going to church instead of the club,

and I strive to be a living example of God's Love.

I walk by faith and not by sight,

so often I sit and meditate all through the night.

I spend time reading my Bible for the spiritual nourishment,

that's needed to provide the world with encouragement.

I'm 5'9" tall and I weigh 183 pounds.

I'm bald, I have big dimples and I'm snicker-brown.

I enjoy working out and writing poems books, and letters,

and I see every day as an opportunity to get better.

I'm the type of man that brightens your life,

because every day I try to be like Jesus Christ.

Made in the USA
Middletown, DE
19 March 2020